How To Make Money From Your Website or Blog

From basics to money in five hours

Philip Copitch, Ph.D.

Author of *Chutzpah Marketing*

Written and illustrated by Philip Copitch, Ph.D.
Printed in the United States of America.

HERE TO SERVE YOU:

Hutzpah Press titles are available in quantity discounts for promotions, premiums and fundraisers.

FOR FURTHER INFORMATION PLEASE CONTACT:

HUTZPAH PRESS
PO BOX 400
IGO CA 96047-0400

Geri Copitch, Sr. Editor
Geri@CopitchInc.com

Dr. Phil's website:
www.CopitchInc.com

Dedication

Thanks Geri, the love of my life!

Tell me, I forget.
Show me, I remember.
Involve me, I understand.

· Table of Contents ·

Introduction

"Uh ... Tell me about your motherboard?"

This book is not about websites or the Internet. It is about how to use your website to the fullest for making money.

This book is about how to Chutzpahize your web presence.

First, what is chutzpah (`huts·pah)? It is boldness coupled with supreme self-confidence. An old Yiddish anecdote illustrates the power of chutzpah:

A man murders his mother and father. Then he throws himself on the mercy of the court because he's an orphan.

Now that's chutzpah!

Chutzpah marketing is business boldness coupled with supreme personal self-confidence. It is the art of doing something right, fairly, and with value.

Business is said to be cutthroat, but that is not what I am teaching. I am talking about being basically lazy and getting a lot done. I want you to do what works, and skip the aggravation of wasted effort. A chutzpah marketer doesn't waste time or money. She works hard and plays hard while loving it all. She has clear goals and follows them. She looks at her options and makes only well informed decisions. Once a decision is made, she does not second-guess herself. She is confident that she did her homework and is now following a sound course of action. A chutzpah marketer can make a decision. She is task oriented and prides herself on task completion.

A chutzpah marketer won't spend a dime if 9¢ will do. But, she is not cheap. She is value minded. When making purchases, she is value conscious. She is future oriented and sees that she is investing in her business, not merely spending money.

A chutzpah marketer is ethical. She carefully abides by the ethical standards of her profession. The ethical standards are incorporated into the very foundation of her business plan.

A chutzpah website is by far the most cost effective and über powerful marketing tool a professional has. Once set up correctly, your website is working for you every second of every day, offering world wide access to your perfectly stated message. As my uncle Sol would say in his thick Yiddish accent, "Vat a deal!"

Just a few years ago, developing a website took specialized computer knowledge or the cash to hire such skills. Now, with just basic computer know-how, you can put together a marvelous website. And, with the information in this book, it is only a little bit more work to go from a marvelous website to a chutzpah website.

If you already have a web guru, the information in this book will help you direct him or her to bring your site into chutzpah drive.

We will start with the basics, where I will demystify the web lingo putting you in the position of knowledge. Then, we will talk about how to start a website from scratch in just a few hours. Finally, the marketing good stuff, I will explain how to use your site for chutzpah marketing.

Remember, in my humble opinion, if you have a business site it has one chutzpah purpose— **To make you money!**

Thank you for encouraging my behavior.

1. Website Basics

"Gramps doesn't know much about the Internet, but <u>he is cool</u>!"

I am going to assume that you have been all over the Internet, visiting lots of sites. You may have even bought something online. Great, with this basic experience we can start our conversation.

You have seen **websites** and played with them, but what are all the parts called? You will need to build a base vocabulary so that you will be able to understand what I am writing about, and so you can explain your needs clearly when it comes time to direct a **web designer**, or when you develop **web content** for your website yourself. In fact, let's start with those 3 web words I just threw out willy-nilly:

> Website: a computer location connected to the Internet that maintains one or more pages on the World Wide Web (WWW).

> Web designer: A person who designs the graphic look of a website.

> Web content: The text, graphics, and links that make up a website. Often simply called content.

A website is made up of one or more web pages, the first page is called the homepage.

> Web Pages: The World Wide Web was initially conceived to connect academics in university settings together. Web Pages initially mimicked typed pages. Now, all content that can be seen on the screen without having to jump to another page is called a web page

> World Wide Web: A widely used information system on the Internet that provides facilities for hypertext

documents to be connected to other documents by hypertext links.

Hypertext: Text displayed on a computer with references (hyperlinks) to other text that the reader can access usually by a mouse click.

Hyperlink: A link from a hypertext file or document to another location, typically activated by clicking on a highlighted word or image.

Homepage: The first page of a website. Programmers call it the index page.

When you surf the net you are using links. Links are made up of **hypertext code** that a **web browser** uses to connect websites.

Surf: The activity of going from website to website.

Links: Links connect two pages of a website together or two websites together. A link is a graphical representation of a computer code that directs your computer to a different part of the website you are in or another website somewhere on the Internet. Hypertext traditionally is shown as underlined blue text. When hypertext is connected to a graphic it is often called a button.

Web browser: A software application for retrieving, presenting, and traversing information resources on the World Wide Web. Common web browsers are:
- Google Chrome
- Microsoft Internet Explorer

- Mozilla Firefox
- Opera
- Apple Safari
- SeaMonkey

Hypertext code: Hypertext Transfer Protocol (HTTP) is the basic computer code that allows computer browsers to communicate. Thus, no matter the make or model of computer, it most likely can share information over the Internet.

Every website on the Internet has an individual address. This address is a specific code number that is given to each website on the Internet. For **web programmers**, a website address is called a **Uniform Resource Locator** (URL).

Web programmer: Individual with the ability to program web pages usually using HTML or similar coding.

Uniform Resource Locator (URL): A web address. It tells the browser specifically where to send you on the WWW.

In actuality, the URL is a highly technical part of the Uniform Resource Identifier (URI). The URI is a set of rules that governs where an identifying resource is on the **World Wide Web** and the mechanism for retrieving it.

Luckily for us we don't have to master that code, but we do need to understand the addressing system, URL. Later in this book we will look at the importance of getting a URL that is helpful to your business, but for now let's look at the parts of a basic

URL.

A basic URL looks like Figure 1.

1. The browser protocol
2. Type of server
3. Name of the website
4. Domain of the site

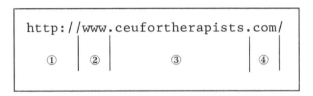

Figure 1: Parts of the web address

The name of the website and the domain make up the domain name.

There are lots of domains available. Common 3 letter domains are:

.COM commercial

.GOV Reserved exclusively for federal and state government

.EDU Reserved for post-secondary institutions accredited by an agency on the U.S. Department of Education's list of Nationally Recognized Accrediting Agencies

.NET Often used by networks

.ORG Often used by public interest organizations

.MIL mostly used for the Department of Defense.

Two letter domains denote countries:

.CA country-code   Canada

.UK country-code   United Kingdom
.GB country-code   United Kingdom
.US country-code   United States
.SZ country-code   Swaziland

One 2 letter country code that is becoming very popular because of its similarity to television is:

.TV country-code   Tuvalu (Ministry of Finance and Tourism) [An island country of the western Pacific Ocean north of Fiji.]

Every domain name in the world ends with a 2 digit country code, except the United States. Since the WWW started here, country codes weren't initially needed. If you want to shop at Amazon.com in England, just direct your browser to http://www.amazon.co.uk/

There are even 4 letter domains, such as:

.MOBI Reserved for consumers and providers of mobile products and services
.INFO Generic top-level domain often used by information sites.

THE PARTS OF THE WEB PAGE

Figure 2 shows the basic parts of a website.

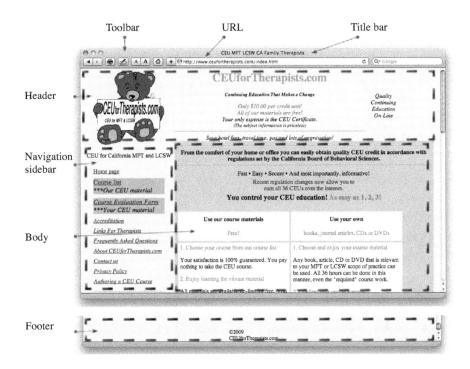

Figure 2: Parts of a website

Header: The top part of the page. It usually consists of the tool bar, URL, and the title page. Many web browsers allow you to customize the header of the web window.

Title bar: This is the title that the web designer gave the page you are looking at. When you start to develop your own web pages, this title becomes very important since it is one of the ways your website is found and defined by search engines like Google and Yahoo.

Tool bar: This is where the navigation tools offered by your browser are kept. The tool bar can be customized.

URL: This is the web address of the web page you are viewing. The URL is typed into the locator window.

Body: This is the content area of the page.

Footer: The bottom part of the page. It usually tells you about the owner or author of the web page. The footer often carries the copyright of the page owner.

NAVIGATING ON A WEB PAGE

What makes a web page more powerful than a piece of paper, is that a web page is dynamic. By clicking on a link, your computer can retrieve and display any public page from any website on the Internet. Most websites make the navigation links easy to find along the top, bottom or left side of the page. It is common, and helpful, when a site has the same navigation link format on every page.

Figure 3 is the NYTimes.com navigation bar found on the left side of every page on their website:

Figure 3: Navigation bar

This is a nice example of a clear and easy to read navigation protocol. By simply clicking on, SCIENCE the Science page of the NYTimes.com website loads into your browser. Words or graphics can be made into links viewed in a navigation bar.

Figure 4 is an example of a Amazon.com search, the **thumbnails** of my books become links.

Figure 4: Thumbnails

Thumbnail: A reduced image of a graphic or document page. Often called *links* or *buttons*.

The graphical aspect of making a link visual, adds a lot to a web page's presentation and eye appeal.

At whitehouse.gov we see a wonderful example of a top page navigation bar with a **drop-down menu**. See Figure 5.

Drop-down menu: Additional links that appear below a menu item when it is selected.

Figure 5: Drop-down menu

When you are navigating from website to website it is as if you are going to the site. In reality, your browser is bringing the site to you, but surfing the web has a feeling of travel that many people find appealing. (If not addictive.) After you click on a link you are sent to what is called a **landing page.**

Landing page: The web page that is retrieved after a link is clicked.

Now you have the basics. Later in this book, we will talk about how to use these basics to build a chutzpah website.

WEBSITE HOSTING

In Chapter 2 of this book I will discuss a few

ways to make and **publish** a website. Once you have your website, you will want the world to be able to see it.

A **web server** is a specialized computer program (system) that is connected to the Internet every second of the day.

> Publish: Placing your website on a web server. Also called upload or put.

> Web server: A program that processes computer document requests. It uses its database to send and receive computer data and website content.

You will need to hire an Internet Service Provider (ISP) to store your website on their server so that it is accessible to the Internet. Over the last few years, ISPs have flourished throughout the world. Competition for accounts, like yours, has helped drop the cost of having your website hosted dramatically.

You own your website, domain name, and all your web content, but you rent your hosting space from an ISP. This is a good thing. For pennies a day, it is someone else's responsibility to keep the web server Internet ready. (A full time, 24 hour a day job.)

Blog

A web**log**, blog, is a chronologically ordered website penned by one or more bloggers (writers). It often allows readers to participate. Throughout this book, the words blog and website are usually interchangeable.

2. Your Company Website

Build Your Own or Hire a Pro?

In the old days, 5 years ago, there were only 2 ways to build a website. You needed to have the coding ability to build a website personally, or you needed to hire someone who had it. This has all changed due to advancements in the Internet and good old American business competition.

When I ask professionals, "Are you planning to build your own website or hire a pro?" I tend to get a guilty look and a statement such as, "I'm an attorney, I don't know how to build a website." Or "My cousin's kid is a computer geek, he built mine for pizza, Mountain Dew, and a hundred bucks." Or "I hired a web designer, I think my site is pretty good..."

All these answers are great, but not necessarily the right answer for the professional chutzpah entrepreneur.

Before I explain, a simple disclaimer: I am going to show you options, and I will name real companies and products. I have no financial stake or endorsement from any of these companies or products.

HIRE A WEB DESIGNER/PROGRAMMER.

Basically a web designer develops the look of a website, while a web programmer writes the code that brings the look of the website to reality. Often they can be one in the same person.

You can find web design companies in your local Yellow Pages or all over the Internet.

Ah, but there is still a big problem. Content. Web developers build websites, but they do not know your business. An experienced web developer can ask you questions and suggest content for your site, but they cannot write your site for you. On the Internet, content is king. You have to grab the eyes of the surfer as they flitter by your site. Then, instantaneously you need to grab their minds. The only way to grab a surfer's mind is with amazing content about your subject. You will need to anticipate your surfer's needs, moods, and desire for your information. More on this in Chapter 3 of this book.

Vincent Flander, the brains behind *Web Pages That Suck* (webpagesthatsuck.com), runs an amusing and educational site devoted to poorly designed websites. As of this writing, webpagesthatsuck.com is 15 years old and not lacking nominations for suck of the day, suck of the quarter, and suck of the year.

Many nominations are for large corporations that spent real money to develop their professional sites. For example:

Worst site contender January-March 2009:

#2 Genicap:

Submitter's comments: I would like to nominate genicap.com. This company is supposed to offer a pretty nice plug-in for Adobe Illustrator; however, I have searched their site for 30 minutes and cannot find out how I can buy a copy. There is no search feature. The navigation SUCKS. It is chock full of technobabble.

#18. MCI Management Center:

Submitter's comments: I find it hard to believe that someone at some point in time found this "cool" and paid for it.

The Daily Sucker #2 for Monday, November 16, 2009 was a web design school:

Submitter's comments: I would like to nominate the following as a website that sucks. This site pleasingly combines overwrought Flash, mystery-meat navigation and weird layout with a complete lack of content.

What the webpagesthatsuck.com site teaches is that it is easier to build a site than it is to build a quality site.

You may want to look at these examples of bad websites:

http://www.manolith.com/2009/08/25/worst-website-designs/

Questions to ask potential web designers

Most web developers know web stuff. They tend not to understand business, and specifically not your business. A few starting questions you should ask:

- Have you built a site for a company like mine?
- If yes, how much did the company's revenue increase because of your site?
- How long will site development take?
- Do you offer hosting packages?
- Do you offer monthly web updating in a package deal?
- What are your views on award winning verses money making site development?

- Are services offered 24/7? (Remember, the web is open 24 hours per day, every day.)

It is very important that you check out any potential developer's work. Study their sites and talk to website owners if at all possible.

And finally, you need to gauge how long employees work for the web design company. Nothing is more vexing and time consuming than having to explain your website to a new developer whenever there is a problem or routine change.

Web content needs to be constantly updated, so it is important to work with someone that you are very comfortable with. If you choose to hire a **web master**, they will become part of your business team, like your accountant or legal adviser.

> Web master: The individual who is responsible for running the website.

BUILD A WEBSITE FROM SCRATCH

If you are the adventurous, and computer problem solver type, you can build a website from the bottom up. Once you know your way around the program, you will have complete control over every **pixel** on every page.

> Pixel: The basic unit of the composition of an image displayed on a computer monitor.

One web entrepreneur made a million plus dollars from controlling every pixel of his website.

Alex Tew built milliondollarhomepage.com, a profit driven website to help pay for college. Published August 2005, Alex sold each pixel for $1.00. On January 1, 2006, the final 1,000 pixels were put up for auction on eBay. The auction closed on January 11 with a winning bid of $38,100. That brought the grand total of the site's income to $1,037,100.00.

There is a tough learning curve to mastering website programming, but once you know it you will have real control over your website.

If you are interested in learning web programming from the ground up I highly recommend the book **Creating a Website: The Missing Manual** by Matthew MacDonald. Second edition (Paperback - Jan 7, 2009) It is a clear, hands-on manual.

BUILDING A WEBSITE FOR NON-GEEK PROFESSIONALS

Most professionals do not have the time or the aptitude to become their own web designer/programmer. And the good news is, you do not have to!

Advances in computer hardware and computer programming has made web building accessible to professionals with just the most basic of computer skills.

Major technology companies are competing for your website dollars. Companies such as Intuit, Yahoo, and Network Solutions offer reasonably priced web packages. Google.sites even offers website hosting for free!

You do not need to know programming, the hosting company offers templates that you get to change by simply pasting in your graphics and text. Many of the companies offer thousands of stock photos and graphics for you to use— royalty free.

These new breeds of business support companies are called **Application Service Providers (APS).**

> Application Service Provider (APS): A company that rents application access (web development tools) which it hosts on its own servers, usually for a monthly fee.

As many mega corporations have built business to business APS companies, the cost of renting the web hosting and development has dramatically dropped. In other words, really huge corporations are fighting to get you to use their computer servers to host your website.

You rent the space and the APS has all the headaches of keeping their product cutting edge. As the web evolves, their products will evolve, but you never have to buy the latest and greatest new program, you just rent what you need.

Each company has its own set of rules and offerings; they tend to bundle together the services that they offer. For example, web hosting, web development, and domain registration for $XX.00 per month.

If you are looking to build an information site about your legal office or your CPA practice, the cost will be under $10.00 per month. If you want a complete web store, with payment gateways and email marketing, the cost will be around $50.00, plus credit card service fees, per month. In a fairly recent development, most of the big players have stopped charging an initial setup fee. (Competition is driving down pricing.)

The following is a short list of some of the well

known APS players:

- www.godaddy.com
- www.smallbusiness.yahoo.com/webhosting
- www.networksolutions.com/web-hosting
- www.ipower.com
- www.intuit.com
- www.inmotionhosting.com
- www.justhost.com
- www.fatcow.com/
- www.land1.com

This is a short list, there are hundreds of APS companies. You will have to go to the sites and see what offers work for your needs. Each company offers slightly different options.

Figure 6: Godaddy.com homepage

For example, godaddy.com (Figure 6) offers links to real stores using godaddy.com hosting services. This way you get to see what real people are doing with the godaddy.com templates. They offer 1,500 website templates to choose from. Godaddy is also a site on steroids. They offer a lot of online products, so the site may feel overwhelming to the first timer. The site is messy and flashy. It has a stripper club-flea market feel to it. All that being so, godaddy.com package deals tend to be very good deals.

Intuit.com (Figure 7) is a very clean and easy to understand site, but it is a little corporate stuffy. If you also want to sell products online, Intuit.com integrates well into their own accounting software. QuickBooks® Integration is offered by many APS at their premium levels.

Figure 7: intuit.com homepage

land1.com (Figure 8) has nice tools but limited templates. They offer hundreds of template choices, while others offer thousands. Their site is messy, making it a little hard to find your choices. Their constantly flashing offers can give you a headache.

Figure 8: 1and1.com homepage

Ipower.com (Figure 9) has lots of templates to choose from and, as of this writing, they are offering free domain names and free setup, starting at under $6.00 per month. They also get a big pat on the back for being green, with all their power coming from wind energy.

Figure 9: Ipower.com homepage

Start slowly for free

If you are unsure, and want to walk to the Internet shore and dangle only a toe in the surf, you can do that for free. Google.com offers free site hosting and lots of helpful information. Most of the introductory information is in the form of short movies (Flash), that show you exactly how to build and manipulate your free website.

Building a site is easy. In less than an hour, you could have a nice site open to all, or viewable by invitation only. If you run into a problem, the site has a comprehensive set of help pages.

When I first went to set up a test site (sites.google.com/site/chutzpahtestsite) I was able to easily change a photo in the center of the page.

When I went to change a photo in the top corner, I got nowhere. The page just refreshed. It wasn't until I realized that the navigation bar had its own setup procedures, that I was able to change the photo in the corner. At the bottom of the sidebar, I found a link How to change this sidebar.

(sites.google.com/site/sitetemplateinfo/tips/customize-your-site-sidebar) This page had clear instructions on how to change all the parts of the sidebar.

So, if sites.google.com is free...

So, if sites.google.com is free why would I want to pay?

Free is good but not always the best choice. The biggest reason has to do with your site's domain name.

My free chutzpah test site at Google sites is:

www.sites.google.com/site/chutzpahtestsite

Not bad for free, but not as professional as my real website: www.CopitchInc.com

My free site makes me look less professional. More on this in Chapter 3: *The Chutzpah Website: What's In A Name.*

Free blog

You can get a free blog hosted by Goggle at: www.blogger.com. This amazingly powerful software is easy to use and easy to monetize. And - I'm not kidding - it's free!

Now let's look at what goes into a chutzpah website.

3. The Chutzpah Website

"Ken loved napping by the glow of his highly monetized website"

A few years ago, a friend who is an anesthesiologist told me that his company just put up their first website.

"You have to you know. Patients want to know where you went to school and what you look like," he explained.

The site the anesthesiologist group put up was just one basic page consisting of the name, school, accreditation, and picture of each doctor. Two doctors didn't want their picture on the site, so in place of their picture, there was a curt notation, "No Picture Available."

There are millions of websites on the Internet as basic as the one described above. After reading this chapter, your website will not be one of them.

A chutzpah website sells! It sells your message, your product, and your company. It brings in customers, gets their attention, answers their questions, and sells them on you. All this for pennies a day; what a deal!

Every aspect of your website needs to be well thought out. Nothing should be on your site unless it adds to your site's ability to sell your company or product. Over the next few pages I am going to explain what to do, and what not to do, to make your website into a chutzpah website.

The most surprising part of developing a chutzpah website is that it is easy. By staying focused on the purpose of your website (sales) and staying away from anything that gets in the way of your focus (sales) you can have a chutzpah site in short order.

YOUR CHUTZPAH WEBSITE FOCUS

The focus of your professional website is to meet the needs of your potential customer. It is important to remember that people go to the Internet for two reasons: education or entertainment. Simply put, they want a question answered or they are looking for fun. If you can give them both you are well ahead of your competition.

Like all of your other marketing, your website marketing must fit perfectly into the business brand that you have developed. A consistent branding between your office or store signage, your advertisements, and your Internet presence is important.

One nice thing about your website is that it is very inexpensive to make it amazing. Color on a website is free. Color in a magazine or a mailer is extremely expensive. Video on a website costs pennies, a 30 second television ad is scarily expensive. Mailing a color brochure to all of your past customers can easily run you $10 per mailer. Having all of your past customers download your amazing, photo filled brochure, will cost you nothing. (For more information on branding and marketing please see my book, **Chutzpah Marketing: Simple Low Cost Secrets For Building Your Business Fortune.**)

Every word you place on the Internet is a form of advertising. What you need to focus on are the benefits you offer to the customer. Let's say you're in the plumbing business or the deli business - so you sell a kitchen sink repair or a pastrami on rye. What did the customer receive? More succinctly, what value did the customer receive?

A customer will only buy your commodities, products, services, or skills if he perceives a benefit to himself that is greater than the cost to his wallet. Customers buy because of perceived value, not because of your skill, item price, or wicked good looks. The sale and all subsequent sales are about the customer. Is the customer getting <u>their needs met.</u>

What businesses like to sell:

- Toaster ovens
- Wills and trusts
- Hamburgers
- Pizza

What customers like to buy, what they value:

- Melted cheese on bread anytime I want it - or maybe a Pop-Tart
- A way to get my kids to go to college and finally make something of themselves
- A cool quiet place to sit down for just a minute and feed the kids so I can get them to soccer by 5pm
- Food that relieves me from having to cook or clean up much

A chutzpah marketer focuses on the needs of the customer. Make sure you talk to, not at, your customer. Solve your customer's problems with words that the customer understands. Use powerful photos, graphics, and video.

The biggest problem with most business websites is that they are written to make the entrepreneur feel good about the important work they do. This type of website is an ego boost for the entrepreneur.

This makes sense because often a web developer or a management consultant *sells* a website to an entrepreneur. These individuals want to keep their customer (you) happy. But, the focus is completely wrong.

The focus of your website should be on your potential customer. The website is your way to *circulate* so you can *percolate.* The website is your representative. What would you teach a potential customer about you if you had their attention? A chutzpah website is a teaching tool and a call to action.

What is the purpose of a business website? It is a sales tool, and hopefully, a chutzpah sales tool. It is not:

- An artistic impression of the warmth of your heart.
- A window into your soul that lets potential clients feel safe.
- A mission statement.
- A vita.

A chutzpah website is a <u>teaching tool</u> and <u>a call to action</u>! You cannot expect your spouse, friends, employees or patients to sell you to a potential customer. However, it is reasonable for any of them to send a link to your website to a potential client and say, "I think this guy can help." That puts a potential customer one click away from your amazing marketing tool. What would you want this referred customer to find when they click on that link?

Actually, before the potential customer gets to your website, they would see your web address. So let's start there. What is a good web address for you?

WHAT'S IN A NAME

In my area there is a wonderful store called Language Quest. It is a cornucopia of books and computer programs to help you learn a new language. Recently, Language Quest has been advertising on local radio that they have added a huge selection of telescopes. The radio ad caught my attention, but over the course of a week, I couldn't *hear* the name of the store. I heard about telescopes, but I didn't *hear* the store's name. I Googled *Meade telescopes Mt Shasta Ca* and found the store. I thought to myself, "Oh, I like that store." Even though I knew of the store, the website didn't stick in my ear when I heard the radio advertisement.

www.languagequest.com

What does Language Quest have to do with telescopes?

I bring this up because when it comes to your website, your domain name counts.

What do you think this company sells?

www.carithers.com

How about this company?

www.1800flowers.com[1]

Both Carithers and 1800flowers sell flowers.

---

[1] 1-800-flowers is also their phone number. This is brilliant!

Which one is easier to remember?

Before you buy your domain name, you want to be very choosy.

Your domain name is a form of company branding. It needs to represent your company's marketing goals and niche. Most of the shortest domain names are already being used. You may have to go to a short declarative statement to get the domain name you want.

All things being equal, it is best if your domain name is short and easy to spell. A domain name has no spaces in it. So, if I want to use my last name, for example, copitch.com[2] while personal to me, it is not very memorable. What is a *co pitch* or a *cop itch*?

How about?

www.drcopitchtherapist.com

What a mess. Without spaces, a reader has no chance to figure out what I'm teaching.

dr copitch therapist

Even worse, what if they read it wrong,

dr co pitch the rapist .com.

I don't think that monicker will be good for my business. Some people try to make their name easier with underlines or dashes. Such as:

great_name.com
great-name.com

---

[2] Pronounced cop•itch

This will prove to be very difficult to say in person or on the radio.

The same is true for tricky word-number combinations. If I'm trying to get to the site about love for cats, is it:

Loveforcats.com or love4cats.com

Plurals are another problem. Is it:

Therapist.com or Therapists.com

If your company name is unique, it can make a great domain name. But it will cost a lot of time and money to teach the public.

The TV show NUMB3RS uses their unique name well. The backwards 3 instead of an E is memorable. If you Google it, it captures the top spots. But if you spell it correctly, it shares the search results with other types of numbers. See Figure 10a and 10b.

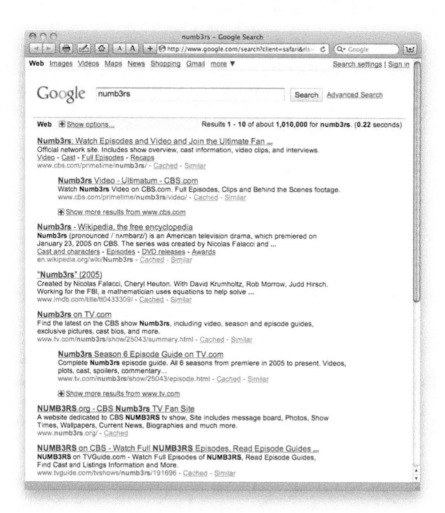

Figure 10a: Numb3rs vs. Numbers search results.

Figure 10b: Numb3rs vs. Numbers search results.

When brainstorming domain names you may find that adding adjectives that help describe the noun will give you more choices. The domain name registration websites can help you with this.

Most of the time your domain name will be in lower case letters. Keep this in mind when deciding on your name.

You will want to avoid contractions and possessive nouns. A domain name can only have letters, numbers, and dashes. So let's say you want to use your company's name for this, and it is *Taylor's Family Counseling*. This works well in print, but not on the Internet. The ' will confuse the Internet. On text pages and in email the ' will often be turned into a box. If you leave the ' off, Taylor's Family Counseling becomes Taylorsfamilycouseling.com. But your name is Taylor, so often your site name will be misspelled.

Three examples of real websites with problematic names as documented by Independent Sources[3]:

1. A site called **Who Represents** where you can find the name of the agent that represents a celebrity. Their domain name… wait for it… is:
www.whorepresents.com

2. **Experts Exchange**, a knowledge base where programmers can exchange advice and views at:
www.expertsexchange.com

3. Looking for a pen? Look no further than **Pen Island** at:
www.penisland.net

Buying your domain name (URL)

You cannot actually buy your domain name, you can only license it. You can license a domain for 1 to 20 years. At the end of the license, you can license your domain name again for 1-20 years. If you do not re-license it, your name can get licensed by anyone who wants it.

URLs are licensed by the rule of first come first served. Companies that license domain names are called registrars. It usually costs $10-$20 per year to license a domain name. The registrars are in competition for your cash so they often offer deals.

---

[3] http://independentsources.com/2006/07/12/worst-company-urls/

Registrars that also offer web hosting tend to offer package deals. Compare:

www.godaddy.com
www.register.com/
www.networksolutions.com

Each of these sites will show you if the domain name you want is available. If it isn't, they will show you a few wording options.

It is best to buy your domain name for more than a year. It tends to be a little cheaper this way, but more importantly, you do not want to take a chance of forgetting to re-register it and losing your valuable URL.

If you are going to go with a package website deal, you don't want to license it for say $10 per year, when you can get it for free in your monthly site fee.

More than one domain name?

You may need more than one domain license. You may want to license common misspellings of your domain name or plurals.

I license copitch.com and copitchinc.com (My business name is Copitch, Incorporated). My main website is www.CopitchInc.com but if you go to www.copitch.com, you are forwarded to www.CopitchInc.com and you don't even know it. Domain forwarding is $10 - $20 per year per domain name. You order it through your ISP. It is often free within a web hosting package.

THE BASIC RULE OF CHUTZPAH WEB PAGE

The basic rule of a chutzpah web page is to tell your story and avoid all other distractions. This rule seems so simple, but it must not be simple, because it is broken constantly.

In all honesty, this is not as straightforward as it seems. You are trying to make a site that represents you and your hard work. You want it to make you shine and your product stand out. The problem with this is that your potential customer doesn't care anything about your needs. They care about their own needs.

Let's say that your customer is looking for a therapist in Their Town. They don't really want a therapist, what they really want is to get their spouse to listen to them and understand their needs better.

This potential customer comes across your website and has to wait as your background music loads and your professional picture downloads. After 30 seconds, your site is loaded and the potential customer scans your site and reads:

- Your name with spaghetti initials after it.
- A quote by Lao-Tsu
- Embarking on a path...
- We will work together to find a treatment mode that works for you.
- Self-discovery is a lonely path, let me be your guide.
- Are you living authentically?

The potential customer looks at the picture of a flower and thinks to herself, "Embark authentically, this person doesn't understand me!" Click, on to the next site.

At the next site, the potential customer finds a picture of a comfortable chair by a window looking out onto a waterfall. As she <u>scans</u> the page, she reads:

- Are you trustworthy and loyal?
- Psychotherapy is not selfish it is helpful.
- Safe and hopeful are the goals for psychotherapy.

The potential customer thinks to herself, "Safe and hopeful, I want my husband to help out more with the kids and to stop drinking all night long in the garage! This therapist doesn't understand my world." Click, and on to a different site.

I purposefully did not show you any particular sites. My goal is not to embarrass or critique an individual's web endeavor. My goal is to help you see that your site must answer clear questions that your potential customer has churning in their mind when they are looking at your site.

When a potential customer lands on your web page, they will scan it, they do not read it. They will scan for information important to themselves. They are looking for ways to get their needs met.

It is imperative that your web page clearly answers your potential customers' needs.

CONTENT IS KING

Because you understand that your website is about meeting the needs of your potential customer, your content is focused on them. When a potential customer lands on your site, they will be getting answers to partially formulated questions that you are helping them solidify. Your potential customer may be thinking, as in the example from earlier, "My husband doesn't listen or seem to care!" But, while scanning your site she may find easy to digest information on how to define her confusing feelings.

Your website offers a very low cost way to disseminate your chutzpah material in the form of a **PDF** such as:

- E-newsletters
- Your chutzpah Waiting Room Resume
- Press releases
- Map to your office or speaking engagements
- Fridge art
- Article reprints
- Menus
- Speaking engagement transcripts
- Photos of you and your staff doing wonderful stuff in the community
- Packets of information on any subject you deem important
- Online coupons
- Links to other websites you consider valuable

PDF: (Portable Document Format) A universal computer file format that preserves fonts, formatting, colors, and graphics in a document. It is readable on any computer with a standard free PDF reader.

Because your website is dynamic you may choose to make audio and video available:

- Audio and video of previous lectures
- Pictures and video of your great work
- Video of you and your staff doing wonderful stuff in the community

The web is limitless!

CHUTZPAH WEBSITE: WHAT TO DO AND WHAT TO AVOID

Landing page

When you set up a link that sends your potential customer to another area of the same page or another web page, it is important that the link does exactly what the user expects. If your link says *Recommended Parenting Books* the link should take the user to exactly that place on the **landing page.** Poorly aimed links will take the reader to say, the top of the page *Recommended Books*, forcing the user to scroll down a long list of all sorts of books to find the *Recommended Parenting Books.*

> Landing page: The web page retrieved when a link is clicked. Where you land after clicking on a link.

In web speak you are hyperlinking to a page anchor.

By using a **page anchor,** you can send your user quickly and exactly to their point of interest. Keeping your potential customers interested in your information helps them feel more comfortable with you.

> Page anchor: A specific tag on a page set as a hyperlink destination.

Quick loading pages

People are basically impatient and they are

really impatient when it comes to surfing the Internet. If a person has to wait even a few seconds longer than "feels" fair to them, they simply show their displeasure by clicking off your site and continue speeding along the Internet super highway. (It is not called "snailing the Internet".)

I have a rule of thumb when it comes to any web page I program. It has to be less than 100 KB, and must load via a telephone modem[4] in less than 10 seconds. What this rule means for all practical applications is that I want my page to pop onto the user's screen no matter how the user is connected to the Internet.

100 KB for a web page can be a lot of information or merely a tiny picture. With a little planning you can get a lot into a 100 KB web page.

Graphics tend to be a big user of web space. A typical digital family snapshot can be 1000 KB or 1 MB. The reason for this hefty size is that when you go to print a digital picture it is a good idea to have at least 300 **dots per square inch.**

> DPI: Dots per inch, a unit of measurement used to describe the resolution of inkjet and laser printers.
> 1 bit A unit of computer information expressed as either a 0 or 1 in binary notation.
> 1 byte A group of computer binary digits or bits (usually eight) operated on as a unit

---

[4] "What?" You say, "People still use modems?" I live in The Country where I don't have access to DSL or other zippy options-much to my sons' chagrin. So, yes, you need to anticipate that some of your potential customers won't have high speed connections to the Internet.

1 KB (Kilobyte) a unit of computer memory or data equal to 1,024 (2^{10}) bytes, or, loosely, one thousand bytes

1 MB (Megabyte) a unit of information equal to 2^{20} bytes or, loosely, one million bytes.

When printing a photo at 300dpi resolution, the printer is able to place 300 dots of color in every square inch of paper. The higher the resolution, the sharper the photo will look.

A computer screen has a resolution of 72dpi. The extra 228dpi are not used by the computer monitor. But, the extra, and unnecessary, 228dpi were still loaded into the user's computer browser only to be discarded by the monitor.

Figure 11 shows a typical Google search page. This page is 48.4 KB in size.

Figure 11: Download activity for a Google search page.

Back in Chapter 1 we looked at the www.ceufortherapists.com homepage (see Figure 2 for larger view)

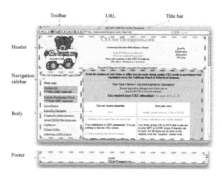

Figure 12: Thumbnail of Figure 2.

Its memory footprint is only 75 KB. It loads quickly, has numerous graphics and a lot of information and background color. If you scroll down, you will find lots more information and 3 more graphics. How, with all this going on, does this page only weigh in at 75 MB? The answer is I used a few web tricks.

The content, what the potential customer is reading to gather pertinent information about you, is memory cheap. If you put a typical 500 page book on a web page, the 2000 letters per page would total about 1 MB of computer memory. Contrast that with a photo of that book used for printing an advertisement to sell the book. A 3 X 5, 300dpi photo would be about 10 MB.

By formatting a picture specifically for your website, you can save a lot. Since the picture will only be seen on a 72dpi monitor, all the extraneous dots per inch can be stripped away. This is called image web optimization. Photo programs such as Adobe

Photoshop use compression algorithms to minimize graphic file size.

Any graphics program can optimize the file size and quality. Optimized web images are usually saved in either GIF, JPEG, or PNG.

By optimizing graphics and using **Flash** animation sparingly, your web page can load quickly. The chutzpah view on this is the quicker the page loads, the quicker the potential customer becomes a new customer.

Minimize Flash

> Adobe Flash: An industry standard program for creating interactive features for websites. Flash looks like animation or a movie in a web browser.

Flash is amazing, awesome, and cool, all rolled into one. If you have ever gone to a site that downloads very slowly or choppily, where the company logo explodes into colors and sounds, and then reintegrates into the company's logo, you have seen Flash. It is great, and graphic designers sell it to company owners to spice up their boring web content.

The problem is that it is a huge memory hog. A 15 second Flash movie can take many minutes to load. Frequently during this loading time the download process takes over the web browser. This often infuriates the user who is trying to get information. (If you want to see an amazing Flash movie of a business icon in all its glory, go the www.adobe.com/products/flashplayer.)

Unless it is integral to your service, Flash does not help your website sell you. I must confess, I have spent hours playing with Flash making my company logo bounce around and explode. However, I am not putting a slow loading, exploding teddy bear logo on my therapy website.

Easy navigation

Make sure that your navigational system is very easy to understand. It is usually best to make the navigation links descriptive.

Website convention is to place the navigation of your site on the upper left side and/or the top and bottom of each page.

You want to avoid using icons as navigation buttons unless they are clearly marked with descriptive labels.

Let's look at some good navigation bars together:

Applied Research Center:

Figure 13: www.arc.org/

Figure 13 shows a top navigation bar. Easy to read—even small. Descriptive labels.

The parents page on the California Polytechnic State University website has a simple and informative left navigation bar (Figure 14). The labels are clear and easy to read.

Figure 14: www.calpoly.edu/student/parents.html

The United Nations welcome page (Figure 15) starts with just the navigation bar. This clear navigation gets you to the UN site in your language.

Figure 15: www.un.org

Check links

Links on the navigation bar, and throughout your website, need to be checked periodically. It is unlikely that a navigation link gets broken by itself, but it does happen. Usually navigation links get corrupted when you are updating site information and neglect to check your newly placed links.

Links that send you to landing pages outside of your site are prone to problems. Recently, I evaluated an attorney's site. When he hired me to help with marketing, he was especially proud of his web presence.

His website was well made but I found 18 broken links. Important parts of his website were broken. For example, on his website he had a navigation link to Press articles/trials. I didn't find this label to be too clear, but the link went to a page of newspaper headlines from local newspapers. Many were broken links because the newspaper had moved or deleted the article from its website. It is better to copy the article and make it available on your website as a free standing page that you control the link to.

In a similar situation, a web designer set up a link *Articles About (Attorney's Name)*. When you clicked on the link the web designer used Google search to build a page of current newspaper article links. This is a nice idea, but a potentially dangerous one. The navigation link automatically searched for the *attorney's name* and the word *attorney*.

When I clicked on the link I was surprised that the attorney who had just hired me had neglected to tell me that he had been indicted in a jury tampering case and was in jail awaiting trial.

As it turned out, an attorney with the same name as my customer, in another state, was a very bad boy. Ah, uh... allegedly.

Links should change colors after being used. This very simple convention is helpful when searching for information. It lets the user know that they have already clicked down that path.

By convention, text links are blue and under-lined; used links are darker red/purple.

If your web page is long enough that the user will need to scroll down, a strategically placed Top of Page link is highly appreciated. With a Top of Page link the user will not have to scroll back up what they have just perused.

Many website designers like to open a new window whenever the user uses a navigation button to a new web page. This way the original page is always left open and just covered by the new page. Users that know how to use their browser's navigation buttons tend to find this bothersome. Your website is taking over their monitor.

I advise that you only open a new page with its own window when the user is leaving your site. That way, your site will be waiting for them when they close the other site's window.

All of your web pages should have the exact same navigation buttons. The user can take themselves wherever they want to go within your site in just one simple click or use their own browser buttons if they wish.

Links should be a call to action. By using a de-clarative statement, the user can read a link and know where the link will take them. A link that says, *Read more,* is nice, but one that says *See Table of Contents*, is better.

Browser navigation buttons

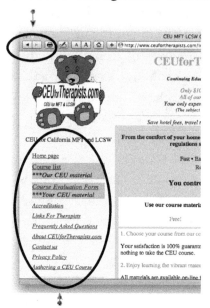

Web site navigation bar

Figure 16: Navigation bars

If you are selling something on your site, don't hide the fact. For example, if you are selling a book called **Fair Fighting Inside Marriage**, a link that says, *Buy Now!* Is clear. If you are not directly selling the book, be clear in the link: *Buy now at Amazon.com.* Users like clear information.

Background colors and white space

White space should be used to make your site easy to scan. Site visitors will not read a treatise. Web users surf, glance and pop around.

(Even though the area is called *white space*, its color does not have to be "white.")

Use white space along with heading, subheading and bullets to control the eye movements of your visitors.

Put the important things first. A chutzpah website is not prose, it is sales. Do not bury the lead. Web users have short attention spans, grab their eyes and minds right at the beginning.

As with a business brochure, your website needs these 5 major parts.

1. A chutzpah headline grabber
2. Powerful subheads that interest the potential customer
3. Dazzling copy that excites the emotions of the potential customer
4. Emotion evoking graphics and/or photos
5. A call to action!

Avoid complicated background colors and design. Do not let anything get in the way of your site's message.

Avoid horizontal scrolling

Scrolling up and down a web page is easy. But scrolling from left to right on a web page is a pain in the mouse. Make sure your web pages are set to be no wider than 12 inches. Ten inches is better.

You want to keep in mind that your web page will be seen on tiny screens like cell phones, up to large landscapes such as High Definition, movie inviting, computer monitors.

Clear contact information

The Internet is often referred to as unruly or

even worse. To combat the appropriate mistrust a user may have for a new site, it is imperative that you give clear contact information.

Links to pages such as: *Contact us*, *Who we are*, or *About us* will get checked and judged by your site visitors.

Do not put any information about you that you do not want every person in the world to know.

If you neglect this web page, you will lose business.

Don't use PDFs for online reading

A common mistake many professionals make is to insert a PDF link where a web page should go. Please let me explain.

If you have a wonderfully made practice brochure, it is very easy to make it into a PDF. With a simple link, you can get your wonderful practice brochure to the curious user's monitor. Web browsers are sophisticated enough to open the PDF in the browser. Now what you have is a representation of your practice brochure plastered on their screen. This is a problem. The PDF is not a web page so it becomes a speed bump on the Internet super highway.

It is much better form to take your practice brochure and re-task it as a real web page, allowing all the conveniences of a real web page. You should also offer a PDF of your practice brochure for them to save or redirect to a friend or family member, in the form of a PDF email attachment.

Use only web safe fonts and colors

For a font to work correctly in a web browser the

font family needs to be installed on the user's computer. There are thousands of fonts available that may or may not be installed on any particular computer. If a browser encounters a web page that possesses a font the receiving computer does not have installed, the browser substitutes the missing font with the closest match that it has access to. This works well most of the time, but sometimes it causes unintended consequences.

Web safe fonts and colors are installed at the factory on every computer sold. Thus, the browser can find web safe fonts on any computer. By using web safe fonts and colors you will get your web pages to be what you expect them to be on every computer receiving it.

For an up to date list of web safe fonts go to:

www.ampsoft.net/webdesign-1/WindowsMacFonts.html

Your website building program will offer web safe pallets to choose from.

It is important to understand that not everyone who will visit your website will have prefect vision. In most likelihood most site visitors will have some form of visual impairment.

Because of this, it is a good idea not to make your web fonts too small. This is harder to do than you may think. **12 point Arial Black is not the same size as** 12 point Courier.

12 and 14 point fonts tend to be good for basic reading.

24 point font is good for headlines.

18 point font makes good subheads.

When it comes to font sizes you get to experiment, but not too much. Too many fonts on a page tend to make a page look cluttered and disharmonious.

Black or very dark font colors work well. It is very popular to put gray fonts or pastel colors on a white background. It may look soothing, but is hard to read for people over the very youthful age of 40.

Soft colors on soft colors is a waste of web space.

Reverse print, white font on black background, is readable as long as there is enough black background to decrease the glow of the rest of the screen.

You want to avoid color contrasts that are difficult for many people to see. As people get older it becomes more difficult to separate the font color from the background color. Thicker fonts will help, but not that much. In addition, thicker fonts are harder to read. Please do not make people work hard to read anything on your site.

SITE MAP OR A SITE INDEX

If your website gets large, say over 100 pages,

or it has a lot of Adobe Flash or Java Script menus, it is a good idea to produce a **site map** or a **site index**. Figure 17 is a site map of Google.com (I assume Google grows every day, so this site map is now outdated.)

Site map: A graphical representation of all pages of a given website showing how they hyperlink.

Site index: Usually a hierarchal listing of all pages of a given website. Sometimes an alphabetical listing of primary website content.

There are two main reasons for producing a site map or site index.

1. It allows savvy web users to navigate your site the way they choose.
2. It allows search engine bots (web crawlers) to find and correctly index all the pages of your site.

Most of us will not need to concern ourselves with site maps or indexes because our sites are small, and our pages are linked by HTML code. Hyperlinked web pages are easily found and cataloged by search engine bots. With navigation bars on every page of your website making navigation simple, even savvy web users won't need to bother with a site map.

Recently, a podiatrist I consulted told me he was talked into paying $280 for a site map of his 11 page website. His web developer told him that it was necessary so the site could get listed on Google. This is untrue. It was simple bill padding by the web developer. If you or your web developer needs to build a website map, Google offers website mapping and diagnostic programs for free.

Go to: www.google.com/webmasters/tools/.

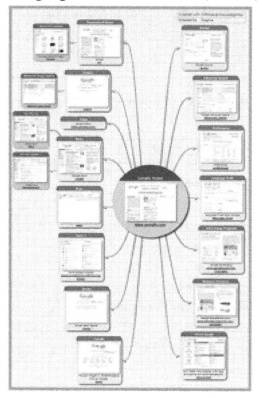

Figure 17: google.com - Site map

COLLECT EMAIL ADDRESSES

It is nice when a potential customer or referral source visits your site. But what makes this contact chutzpah special is if you have a way to keep in contact with this visitor.

To do this you will need to get the visitor to give you their email address along with their permission for you to occasionally contact them.

This isn't as hard as it sounds. All you need to do is offer the visitor a free download, such as an amazingly informative newsletter, or a free packet of must have information. I have an attorney friend that offers free information on what to say to the police if you are stopped, or just what *are* the California laws concerning marijuana? Low cost to produce, and a must have PDF.

Enticing buttons such as:

Please sign up for...

Free newsletter - Sign Up Now!

Reading list every parent needs to know about

Know your rights! A free mini download to keep in your wallet or purse

Please sign our Guest Book

If your web content is compelling, visitors will want more information and be willing to give you permission to contact them.

Remember to clearly state your policy concerning use of private information. The following privacy policy shows how information is used at CEUfortherapists.com

PRIVACY POLICY

Our privacy policies are simple.

CEUforTherapists.com does not sell or otherwise reuse any information gathered from its students except as stated below...

CEUforTherapists.com will use your personal information to verify to licensing agencies, as mandated by said agencies, that a student has completed CEUs.

CEUforTherapists.com will email students brief course information and program offerings. Any student can opt-out of this email information by replying to it with the word "unsubscribe" in the email subject box. CEUforTherapists.com will gladly remove the student's email address from the email database.

CEUforTherapists.com has no control over the privacy policies of other websites. If you choose to link through the CEUforTherapists.com website to another website, please consult that website's privacy policies. Links to other websites are intended as public gateways.

A clear policy, and a clear opt-out rule, goes a long way in building Internet trust.

SEARCH ENGINES AND YOUR WEBSITE

I would like to give you a brief overview of the most important, and often overlooked, aspects of a website. The parts of your website that gets your site noticed by search engines such as Google, Yahoo, or the newest, Bing.

>>>Please be forewarned, the rest of this chapter is a little geek intense.<<<

Web search engines let you search by keywords for information you are interested in. Search engines make no money off your searches. Their goal is to get people to come to them for their information needs. The way the search engine makes money is by selling **pay-per-click** advertising to companies that hope you are looking for what they have to offer, based on your search parameters.

> Pay-per-click: A web based marketing system in which the advertiser pays only when a user clicks on its advertisement and goes to the company's website. Often the web advertisements are shown to the user based on what the user is viewing, or via keywords used in a web search.

The search engines send out information gathering programs called robots (bots), web crawlers, or spiders. These programs make downloads of every site page they come across, eventually even yours.

Once the information is downloaded, the search engines electronically dissect the millions upon millions of web pages, filtering out pertinent information that they catalog to form their search results.

This filtered information concerning your website comes directly from your website. Thus, you have total control over what the search engines can or cannot find.

For example, in Figure 18, I searched for "CEU for Therapists" and Google returned its results (See label 1). In .46 seconds Google found over 1 million web pages that met my search criteria (See label 6).

Google used parts of the site to fill in the search results. The web page title leads off the search result. Here I used the **keywords** that most represent the needs of my potential website user, psychotherapists looking for online continuing education units. The web page title should consist of the most important keywords or phrases. (CEU MFT LCSW CA Family Therapists).

Figure 18: Parts of the basic search engine window

KEYWORD

Keyword: A word or phrase used to limit an Internet search.

The page meta tag is my site page description:

From the comfort of your home or office you can easily obtain quality CEU credit in accordance with regulations set by the California Board of Behavioral...

The last part of the search result is the website domain name: www.ceufortherapists.com/. This points out the importance of a descriptive domain name.

The four main website meta elements

Meta[5] elements are computer code placed in the HEAD of an HTML or XHTML web page that gives information to a search engine that is usually not accessible or noticed by the website user. These tags are important for chutzpah marketing because we get to place the specific words or phrases that define our website's uniqueness from the hundreds of millions of other websites on the Internet. There are 4 major meta elements that help your site get noticed. If you are not familiar with web programming, the following may seem confusing. I have put it here as a reference for your web planning.

Document title

```
<title>
```
The <title> element holds the title of the web page. The web page title is displayed at the top of the web page window in the title bar.

```
<title>CEU MFT LCSW CA Family Therapists</title>
```

Meta description

```
<meta>
```
Embedded descriptive information for search engines to find and catalog.

---

5 Meta is Greek for transcending. In computer speak it means "more than the usual."

```
<meta name="description" content="From the comfort
of your home or office you can easily obtain quality
CEU credit in accordance with regulations set by
the California Board of Behavioral ..."/>
```

Meta keywords

```
<meta>
```
Embedded descriptive information for search engines to find and catalog.

```
<meta name="keywords" content="CEU, continuing
education unit, MFT, LCSW, CA, California, Fam-
ily Therapists, licensed marriage and family thera-
pists, licensed clinical social worker, approved by
board of behavior health examiners, approved by
BBS"/>
```

Words and phrases that are placed into your keyword meta tag also need to be sprinkled throughout
your website content. By matching your keywords to
your page content, search engine computers can separate your site from SPAM sites. Spammers notoriously
use keyword elements to trick search engines into
mislabeling the spam site.

Image

```
<img>
```
This tag defines the name of the image and the
alternative text of the image. Using descriptive
words for an image allows a search engine to index
the image. For example, if your company logo is
called *company logo*, that may be descriptive enough

in your computer, but not on the Internet.

> <img src="images/TB-CEUforTherapists-LOGO-200.jpg" alt=" CEU for therapists logo of teddy Bear holding sign that reads CEU for California MFT and LCSW" height="209" width="200">

All image tags have an *alt* element part. This stands for alternate text. If the image does not load, or if the image is being read to a visually impaired user, the *alt* text is substituted or spoken. Also, search engines use "alt=" tags on your site to verify the veracity of your website.

Some web browsers display the *alt* text to web users when they hover the mouse pointer over an image.

4. Monetizing Your Website

MONETIZING?

Monetizing means the act of making money with your website. Specifically it means making ongoing passive income with your website.

Monetizing: Making money with your website.

If you own a candy shop at the mall, the most likely goal of your website is to encourage customers to purchase candy from your brick and mortar store and/or to order candy directly from your website which you subsequently mail to your customer from your store. This form of **E-commerce** is **active income.** The customer orders a product or comes into your store to buy a product. You actively need to sell the product or ship the product.

E-commerce: Commerce that is conducted electronically, as over the Internet.

Your website also offers the opportunity for **passive income.** Passive income is income made from non physical labor. Traditionally, passive income referred to earnings from stocks, bonds, rental income, or interest form certificates of deposits.

Passive income: Income made from non physical labor.

Active income: Income made from labor, usually physical or time consuming labor.

In the digital world a new form of passive income has developed — web page advertising called affiliate advertising. Figure 19 is a basic example.

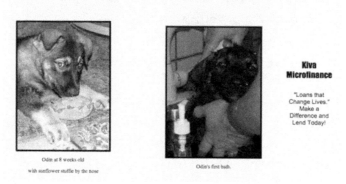

Copitch Family Pets and Furry Friends (And not so Furry)

Kiva
Microfinance

"Loans that
Change Lives."
Make a
Difference and
Lend Today!

Odin at 8 weeks old
with sunflower stuffie by the nose

Odin's first bath.

Figure 19: Passive income advertisements.

On my website I have a page of photos showing my pets and the wild critters in my backyard. Figure 20 shows part of the web page http://www.copitchinc.com/copitch_pets_and_critters.htm.

If a visitor to this web page clicks on any ad, the advertiser will pay me a few pennies to many dollars. I'll explain how this works in a moment. But, I want you to take a minute and think about this form of passive income.

I have this page on my website because I like the critters in my backyard. Other people also like to see pictures of the critters in my backyard. This is unique content to my website. If you want to see a picture of my wolf friend Odin at 8 weeks of age, you need to go to this web page. And, as it turns out, lots of people want to see how Odin grows up. (Grow is the operative word, Odin is now 161 lbs.) The same is true for my rattlesnake friends and the bears and lions that wander by my mountain home. Figure 20 shows unique content only found at my website. As we discussed earlier, content is king!

Cougar in front yard tree.

We don't see cougars often. This young lady visited for about half an hour, then went on her way.

Figure 20: Unique content.

On another page (Figure 21) of my website (http://www.copitchinc.com/downloads.html), I have PDF files available as free downloads. These free downloads are coloring pages we call "Fridge Art" that children like to crayon. I also offer forms and activities from my books so digital readers or listeners to the audio book versions can get a physical copy by downloading and printing the PDF. This is free content that I am happy to give out to anyone who wants it. I want to make this unique content available to my readers, and if it also makes me a few pennies of passive income… great!

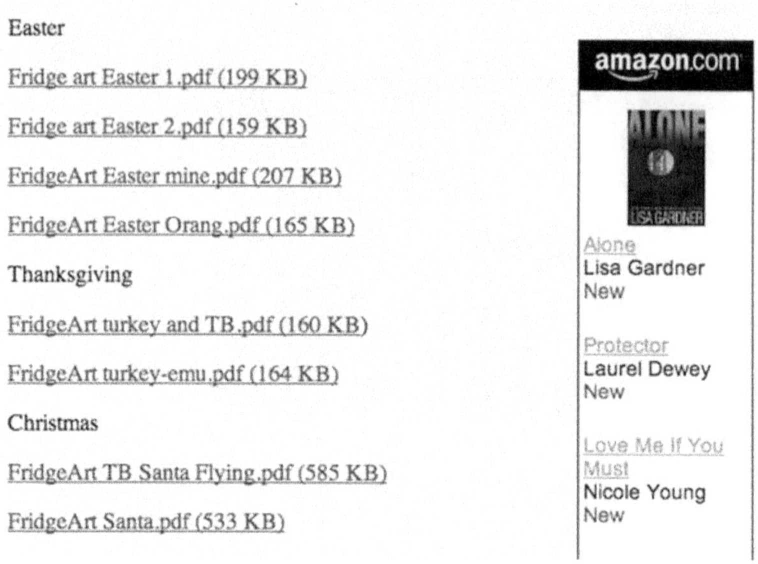

Easter

Fridge art Easter 1.pdf (199 KB)

Fridge art Easter 2.pdf (159 KB)

FridgeArt Easter mine.pdf (207 KB)

FridgeArt Easter Orang.pdf (165 KB)

Thanksgiving

FridgeArt turkey and TB.pdf (160 KB)

FridgeArt turkey-emu.pdf (164 KB)

Christmas

FridgeArt TB Santa Flying.pdf (585 KB)

FridgeArt Santa.pdf (533 KB)

amazon.com

ALONE

LISA GARDNER

Alone
Lisa Gardner
New

Protector
Laurel Dewey
New

Love Me If You
Must
Nicole Young
New

Figure 21: Free downloads as unique content

Affiliate marketing

Affiliate Marketing is a form of advertising where a business rewards another business for sending them customers. In the old days, 1990, this was often simply called payment for a referral or lead generation. In the quickly changing format of the Internet, Affiliate Marketing is in its infancy, but the democratic nature of the Internet lets everyone play if they want to.

> Affiliate Marketing: A web marketing practice in which a business rewards a website owner for each visitor or customer brought about by the website owner's own marketing efforts.

The subject of Affiliate Marketing is easily a business course unto its self. In this section, I'm going to teach you the basics so that you can start getting some passive income from your website. The really nice thing about affiliate marketing is that it is basically easy to do from the comfort of your home or office with just a little knowledge and experience.

There are a lot of ways to use affiliate marketing with your website. Unfortunately, as is often true concerning making money, there are also affiliate marketing schemes that you need to be cautious about. In this section I am going to explain the safest two companies to work with to set up your affiliate marketing. As you progress in affiliate marketing, you may want to explore other affiliate marketing groups. But please be cautious.

The two companies that I highly recommend as being safe, which I use myself, are Amazon Associate and Google AdSense.

A FEW MARKETING WORDS TO UNDERSTAND

In the world of affiliate marketing there are a few words that are bandied about that confused newcomers. Take a moment to understand the following definitions and you will no longer be a newbie.

Associate: What Amazon.com calls affiliate marketers.

Affiliate: What everyone calls a web referral marketer except Amazon.com

Note: In the average brick and mortar business, an **associate** or an **affiliate** are usually called sales representatives or simply sales reps. The biggest difference is that in the digital world the associate or affiliate tends to be an independent contractor working for themselves, whereas the sales rep tends to be an employee of the company.

In the present environment of the Internet, the labels *affiliate, associate, or sales representative* are actually inadequate. It is much more literal to think of these sales people as entrepreneurs. In the traditional business model the sales rep sold the company's products. In the Internet sales model, the entrepreneur is the company. The associate or affiliate choses what product they wish to represent to this audience.

The website owner has a relationship with this web content consumer. Based on this relationship, the website owner tells their content consumer that they can trust the products advertised on their site.

> Publisher: The person who publishes a website, web page, or blog.

> Developer: A large publisher, often running hundreds or even thousands of websites, usually with customized computer programs.

Seeing you own your website, you get to choose what product to present to your website visitors. The basic sales process of affiliate marketing is amazingly simple. You choose what products to present to your website visitors and when they buy you receive a share of the product's price. Once you get the hang of this and your site visitors numbers are soaring, you can get very creative in the ways you get paid, but for our purposes here, we are going to see how to set up a safe and reliable selling environment with companies that have a trustworthy track record. Let's look at working with Amazon and Google.

AMAZON ASSOCIATE

https://affiliate-program.amazon.com/

Amazon.com offers an easy and well organized process to help you monetize your website (Figure 22).

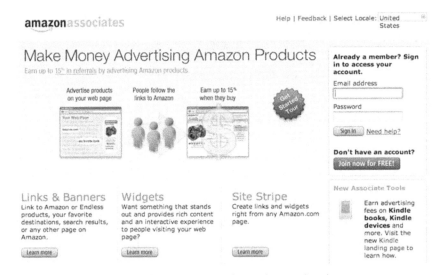

Figure 22: Amazon.com Associates sign in page

You place an ad for an Amazon product on your web page, and if someone clicks-through the ad and actually buys a product, you receive a small part of that sale.

Amazon makes it easy for you to present your web visitors a nice advertisement by writing the computer

code for you, that you add to your web page. At
first, this sounds complicated but it really is simply cut and paste. Amazon embeds your unique associate number into the HTML computer code making sure
you will be credited with the sale.

Amazon pays 4-8.5 percent of the product sale to
start. The rates are constantly in flux and new programs are regularly added. You will find the complete
payment information in the Associates Program Advertising Fee Schedule which is part of the Operating
Agreement that governs your participation in the Amazon Services LLC Associates Program. Amazon companies
Endless.com and Smallparts.com presently pay 15 percent.

Get started with Amazon Associates Program

From the Amazon introduction:

With our simple tools, you can choose
several ways to link to Amazon.com and
Endless.com from your site.

To add compelling content and enhance
your site, you can customize <u>Links</u>,
<u>aStores</u> and <u>Widgets</u>. Simply browse and
select the type of product you'd like to
add, then follow instructions to get
started. (See Figure 23.)

Figure 23: Amazon Associates basic plan

You start by opening a free account with Amazon. (https://affiliate-program.amazon.com/) The site is well designed and set up to teach. Bring a big cup of coffee and plan on taking the time to do the tutorials. Within an afternoon you will be able to choose a product that you think your website visitor will be interested in, obtain the code, paste it into your website, and presto you have monetized your web page.

GOOGLE ADSENSE

www.google.com/adsense

From the beginning, Google AdSense offers you click-through payment. If a visitor to your website clicks on a Google ad, you get paid. Not much, but the pennies can add up.

With Amazon your website visitor has to buy something for you to get paid, with Google you get paid if they show interest in an ad and click on it. (You are not allowed to click on your own website ads.)

From the stand point of the company who placed the ad, a curious consumer wanting more information about their product is a very desirable prospect.

Google decides what type of ad to place on your website based on your web page content. So, if your web page content is devoted to German Shepard Dogs, your AdSense ads will tend to be dog related. If your content is devoted to Babies and Child Care you can expect diaper and children's clothing ads. Google will judge your web content and attempt to present ads your visitor may be interested enough in to click on. If the Google algorithms cannot categorize your web page, you will get very general ads.

The more specific the ads are for your visitor, the more likely they will catch the reader's attention and encourage them to click… placing money in your account.

How does Google AdSense work?

How much you get paid for a click-through depends on the individual click-through ad. Goggle offers advertisers the ad space based on keywords that the advertisers bid for. This is usually referred to as a **cost-per-click** or CPC rate. Some keywords are very desirable so advertisers pay a lot for them in a polite online bidding war mediated by Google. Other words are quite mundane, so advertisers do not fight to get those words. The more desirable the keyword, the more your piece of the click-through action will be. (I will discuss this issue more in a moment.)

> cost-per-click (CPC): The site owner is paid when a website visitor clicks on an ad.

Google attempts to match the ads presented on your web pages to the potential reader of your page. This way everyone wins. The advertiser gets viewers that have shown an interest in their type of product, and the web visitor gets shown products that they may actually want to know more about.

If your site becomes very popular, Google may offer you **cost-per-mil** ads or CPM. Mil is short for the Latin word mīlle, one thousand. Once your site is getting lots of eyes on it, Google may choose to pay you just to show their ads, X amount per thousand viewings. This is a big reason why the major TV networks, radio stations, and newspapers constantly invite you to "get more information by" visiting their sites.

> cost-per-mil (CPM): The site owner is paid when Google shows an ad a total of 1000 times to your site visitors.

To get started with Google AdSense

To get started with Google AdSense you need to apply for an account. Accounts are free and the Google website is well designed, making it easy to figure out the process. Start at:

www.google.com/adsense

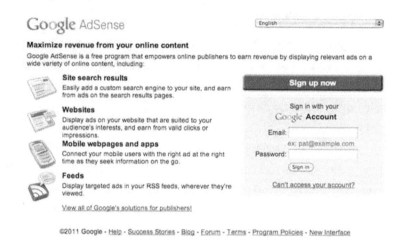

Figure 24: Google AdSense welcome page

As I suggested with Amazon, grab yourself a big cup of coffee and enjoy the tutorials that Google offers. Most of the tutorials are video how-to's and are very well done. Both Amazon and Google want you to become very savvy users of their tools. Remember, they get paid when you get paid.

INCREASING YOUR WEBSITE'S PASSIVE INCOME

Up to now I have been sharing the very basics of monetizing your web presence. In this section I will discuss how to get a little bit more bang for your monetizing effort.

Not all ads are created equally

Advertisers are paying Google and Amazon to find them paying customers. If you think about that for a moment, readers of your web content are their paying customers.

Your content uniqueness is important to the advertisers. If your website is about collecting toy cars your ads will most-likely be about toys and toy cars. If your site is about collecting 1950 muscle cars your ads will most-likely be about real cars. Advertisers for $50,000 real cars are more likely to compete at a higher dollar amount in the key word bidding than advertisers that sell $4.99 toy cars. Since you get a small piece of the action, if appropriate, have your content discuss higher priced items.

Please let me give you an example.

In my December 9, 2010 blog, Stump the Shrink http://stumptheshrink.blogspot.com, I wrote about why people tend to exaggerate problems. The Google AdSense ads were for herbal supplements. This type of ad pays 4 to 10 cents per click through.

In my August 11, 2010 posting entitled What should a parent do if their child steals? The Google algorithms presented ads for safes and home security systems. One click-through for a safe garnered $17. It takes a lot of herbal supplement click-throughs to equal a safe click-through.

When I am writing content for my websites, I do not focus on the ad CPC potentials. I focus on the subject matter that is important to me and hopefully my loyal readers. However, if I am going to give an example as part of my prose, and two pop into my head, one on toy cars and one on Lamborghini race cars, I'm going with the Lamborghini example. I would guess that a Lamborghini ad has a pretty sweet cost-per-click.

Getting web traffic

Web traffic is the term used by website publishers and developers to discuss the amount of web surfers that click onto a particular site. In this section we are going to discuss the basic process of getting people to visit your site.

> Web Traffic: The amount of data into and out of a website.
>
> Website Analytics: The measurement of the behavior of visitors to a website.

There is a growing science of web metrics that is being developed and verified. This web analytics is increasingly important as companies of all sizes try to understand the potential value of websites. In its simplicity, the goal is to figure out what can be done to make passive money from a website. At this point in our website development, we are going to look at how to get visitors to our site. I have broken the discussion down into two categories: low or no cost traffic development and pay-to-play traffic development.

Know your site stats for free

Google offers a sophisticated and free overview of your website. Start with the videos at the link *Google Analytics in 60 Seconds by googleanalytics*. It is a wealth of information and all free. These ten videos, each less then 2 minutes in length, will take 16 minutes to watch.
See them at
www.youtube.com/view_play_list?p=85CE2D27BC6FD84B.

(Note: GA = Google Analytics)

1. GA in 60 Seconds: Using Site Search
2. GA in 60 Seconds: Tracking Ecommerce with Google Analytics
3. GA in 60 Seconds: Improve Location Targeting
4. GA in 60 Seconds: Find Poor Performing Campaigns and Keywords
5. GA in 60 Seconds: Find the Best Keywords
6. GA in 60 Seconds: Linking AdWords & Analytics
7. GA in 60 Seconds: Identifying High Spenders
8. GA in 60 Seconds: Placement Targeting
9. GA in 60 Seconds: Conversion Funnels
10. GA in 60 Seconds: Segment AdWords Traffic

Low or no cost traffic development

If the world was a perfect place and chocolate was not fattening, you would simply build a wonderful site and millions of eager visitors would flock to it to sample your offerings. But, in reality for most people, the world is full of uncountable options, with just one option being to visit your site.

The nice part of this story is that people will come to your site, all they have to do is know about it. In this section we will look at the basic ways to get the word out about your site. And, for almost nothing. Now that is chutzpah marketing.

The top chutzpah ways to get web visitors for little or no cost:

1. Have a website address that is easy to read and understand. (See: **Chapter 3. The Chutzpah Website**)

2. Your website address gets printed on everything your company prints: stationary, business cards, fliers, reports, brochures… everything!

3. Add your website address to the stationary section of every email your company sends. (Emails are often redirected by others and your website address will get bounced around the world for free!)

4. Give prominent placement to your website address in every advertisement or promotional item your company develops.

5. Ad your web address to all social media profiles such as Facebook and LinkedIn.

6. Swap website links and/or ads with friends and colleagues. ("I'll put your company link on my website for free if you will offer me the same courtesy.")

7. When you comment on another website, such as in a book review or an opinion comment, add your web address after your name; such as, Philip Copitch, Ph.D., CopitchInc.com

8. When you are interviewed for a print or web publication, specifically ask for your web address to be part of your profile. This is common and most publications will gladly honor your request.

9. Use 9-second speeches to direct others to your website. Such as:
   · "On my website I have a free download called, *What Every Parent Needs To Know About Street*

Drugs. Here's my card, the website address is printed here," (as you hand them the card)

· "We offer Continuing Education classes. The course material is free at my website, CEUforTherapists.com, It's printed here…" (as you hand them the card)[6].

10. When you give a presentation or lecture, make your web address a visual aid and a handout.

Pay-To-Play traffic development

Do the following only after you have done the free or low cost ideas presented above. Pay-To-Play can get very expensive.

1. Advertise with Google AdWords. (https://services.google.com/advertisers/us)

2. Develop and build an opt-in email marketing campaign. For more info see: http://www.constantcontact.com/index.jsp

3. Use promotional items such as imprinted pens, shirts, or caps to specifically promote your website. This can often get expensive, but many companies share the cost for promotional items between their general advertising budget and their website development budget.

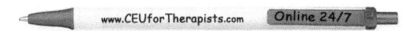

---

[6] More on 9-Second Speeches can be found in my book *Chutzpah Marketing: Simple Low Cost Secrets For Building Your Business Fortune* available at http://store.copitchinc.com/

4. Offer web only coupons that can only be obtained from your website or can only be used at your website.

5. Produce a video to promote your website or a product. Host the video for free on YouTube.com. There is lots of free help available - most in short video format. (http://www.youtube.com/user/YouTubeHelp) As the world gets more digitized, I suspect that more teaching will be done this way.

In Closing

In this day and age it is imperative that you have a web presence. I hope that this introduction has given you the tools you need to put yours on the web—with chutzpah style!

Please let me give you a warning about the web. Be cautious about who you pay to help you. If it is too good to be true, please quickly click off their website.

Have a question or comment? Please feel free to contact me by email at DrPhil@CopitchInc.com.

Check out my company websites at:

www.CopitchInc.com

www.CEUforTherapists.com

www.chutzpahmarketing.com

Books, ebooks, and audio books by Dr. Copitch:

http://store.CopitchInc.com

Also available at:
- www.Amazon.com
- And on Amazon Kindle and the Apple iBookstore for the iPad and iPhone as well as other smart phones.
- www.Smashwords.com